TORMEAD LIBRARIES

**This book is the property of
TORMEAD SCHOOL.**

Please make sure you have issued
the book correctly to yourself on
the library computers, or signed it
out on the blue sheet.

Loan period
The book is due back three weeks
after you borrowed it, or earlier if
you have finished with it.

Renewals
The librarian will renew the book
on request if no one else has
reserved it.

Please take care of this book. You
will be asked to pay for any loss or
damage.

STEP-UP
SCIENCE

Habitats

Louise and Richard Spilsbury

Evans

Published by Evans Brothers Limited
2A Portman Mansions
Chiltern Street
London W1U 6NR

© Evans Brothers Limited 2007

Produced for Evans Brothers Limited by
White-Thomson Publishing Ltd,
Bridgewater Business Centre,
210 High Street,
Lewes, East Sussex BN7 2NH

Printed in China by New Era Printing Co. Ltd

Project manager: Harriet Brown

Designer: Flick, Book Design and Graphics

Consultant: Jackie Holderness,
educational consultant and writer

British Library Cataloguing in Publication Data

Habitats. – (Step-up science)

  1. Habitat (Ecology) – Juvenile literature
  591.5'64

ISBN-13: 9780237532086
ISBN-10: 0237532085

Acknowledgements:

The authors would like to thank Scott Fisher,
teacher at Stokenham Area Primary School for his
invaluable comments and advice on this series.

Picture acknowledgements:

Martyn f. Chillmaid: page 16. CORBIS: page 7
(Stuart Westmorland), 25bl (Stephen Frink).
Ecoscene: page 27r (Paul Ferraby). Istockphoto:
cover (all), pages 1, 5t, 6, 8b all, 9b, 11c, 11t, 12b,
14t, 14b, 17, 18t, 19, 20–21, 22b, 23t, 24, 25tr,
27l, 28 all, 29 all. Natural Science Photos: pages 4
(R. Revels), 9t (R. Revels), 10t (Stephen Davis).
NHPA/Photoshot: pages 5b (Stephen Dalton), 8t
(Manfred Danegger), 10–11 (Stephen Dalton), 12t
(Daniel Heuclin), 15t (Martin Harvey), 18b (Gerald
Cubitt), 21b (Stephen Dalton). OSF/Photolibrary:
page 22t (Oxford Scientific). Photolibrary: pages 13
(Alain Dragesco-Joffe C/O Efital Photography), 15b
(Gustav Verderber), 23b (Mike Birkhead). Science
Photo Library: page 21t (Jim Zipp). Topfoto: page
26 (Topham/Chapman).

Illustration by Ian Thompson (page 11b).

Contents

What is a habitat?

A habitat is a place where plants and animals live, such as a woodland or a pond. Habitats provide living things with all that they need to survive. Living things are also called organisms. Organisms need food to make energy to grow and to live. They need water to drink and air to breathe. They also need space and a place where they and their offspring (babies) can shelter from bad weather and dangerous animals.

Different habitats

Organisms are found in different habitats across the world. They are found in habitats of all sizes, from giant rainforests or deserts to small habitats like a garden or a pond. Small habitats can also exist within larger ones. For example, the space beneath a rock or the surface of a rotting log can be a mini habitat for plants and small animals within a wood. A rock pool is a small habitat within the larger habitat of a beach.

Describing habitats

Even though you may not have visited many different types of habitat, you may be able to describe them.

Match the descriptions to the three habitats.

FOREST

BEACH

MOUNTAIN

wet

sandy

high

shady

cold

damp

dark

windy

snowy

◄ A dead, rotting log can be a busy habitat. These stag beetle larvae feed and live on dead wood for up to seven years.

◀ Choose three words that accurately describe the habitat in this picture.

Habitat conditions

Different habitats have different physical conditions. These conditions include the temperature (how hot or cold it is) and the type of ground (whether it is wet or dry). A polar habitat is cold, icy and dry, while a desert habitat is sandy, rocky, hot and dry. Can you think of any other words to describe conditions in two different habitats?

Plans

Make a plan of a garden or an area around your school, to show the many different mini habitats found there. You might include a garden wall, a tree, a flower bed, a hedge, a pond and a log pile. Describe how each habitat is different and name some organisms you could expect to find there.

▲ These mites (x2 their normal size) are living in bread flour. The mini habitat provides the mites with food, shelter and a place to breed.

Classifying living things

Knowing how organisms are classified (grouped together) helps us to identify them and understand why they live in particular habitats.

Classifying plants

Plants are divided into two groups: flowering plants and non-flowering plants. Flowering plants all have flowers, but come in a wide variety of shapes and sizes. Trees, grasses and dandelions are all flowering plants. The flower is the reproductive part of a plant, where seeds are made. Seeds can eventually grow into new plants. Non-flowering plants, such as ferns and mosses, are often smaller than flowering plants and live in shady, damp habitats.

Classifying animals

Animals are divided into two groups: vertebrates (animals with a backbone) and invertebrates (animals without a backbone). Invertebrates are mini-beasts that include worms, spiders, slugs and centipedes, and insects such as flies and beetles.

Ferns and mosses are types of non-flowering plant. By this stream, the fern (bottom right) is growing in the soil and the moss is growing on the rocks.

Vertebrates

- Mammals **have hair or fur and feed their young on milk. Mice and deer are mammals.**

- Birds **have wings and feathers, and hatch from hard-shelled eggs. Robins and eagles are birds.**

- Reptiles **have hard, scaly skin and hatch from soft eggs. Snakes and lizards are reptiles.**

- Amphibians **hatch from eggs underwater but the adults live on land. Frogs and toads are amphibians.**

- Fish **have soft, scaly skin and can only live in water. Pike and trout are fish.**

▼ *These starfish and anemones have adapted to live in saltwater seashore habitats. They would die in a field, forest or freshwater pond.*

Adaptations

Within each group of plants and animals there are many different types. Each has special features that help them to live in their habitats. These features are called adaptations. For example, some fish have adapted to live in salty ocean water, while others only survive in freshwater ponds and lakes. Some flowering plants live on chilly mountain tops, while others can only survive in warm, moist forests. Most organisms have only adapted to live in one or two types of habitat.

Worms and snails

Find three earthworms and three snails. Gently place them in a plastic container. Create one damp, stony habitat with some fresh grass, and one soil habitat with bits of old leaves in it. What do you discover? Why do you need to use more than one sample of each animal? Remember to put any organisms back where you found them.

Finding food in habitats

In some habitats, a great number and variety of organisms live close together. Fortunately, they often eat different types of food. They have adaptations that help them to reach, catch or trap it.

Eating different foods

Some animals, such as tigers, lions and great white sharks have strong, sharp teeth for grabbing and biting animal prey. Many insects, including butterflies, have a tube-like mouth called a proboscis, which they poke into the centre of flowers to suck up sweet nectar. In African grasslands, zebras and wildebeests have flat teeth to munch grass on the ground. Elephants have long trunks and giraffes have long necks to reach tree-top leaves.

▲ A blackbird has a long, pointed beak for pulling worms out of the ground.

Birds and beaks

Birds' beaks have adapted to eat different foods. Some birds have small, narrow beaks to pick up and eat insects such as caterpillars. Some rainforest birds have large, strong beaks that can crack open tough nuts. Long, spear-like beaks are good for catching fish and birds of prey have sharp, hooked beaks for tearing into flesh. Can you match the bird and beak with the right food?

◀ *Foxes stalk small animals such as mice. How do you think a fox's ears help it to catch prey?*

Predators and prey

Animals that hunt and eat other animals for food are called predators. The way a predator catches its food depends on its prey and its habitat. A fox in a meadow stalks rabbits by sneaking up on them slowly, hiding in long grass until it is ready to pounce. A frog uses camouflage. Its skin is green and brown to blend in with the colours in its habitat. It lies in wait and then flicks out its sticky tongue to catch insects, snails and worms as they pass by. Some prey animals use camouflage to protect themselves. How would a mountain hare's white fur protect it from predators during winter?

Draw and learn

Find a photo of a plant or animal on the Internet or in a book, or find the real thing in a garden or park. Carefully observe the plant or animal you have chosen, and then draw it as accurately as you can. Don't worry too much if your drawing doesn't look exactly like your subject. You will learn a lot about how it works, just by looking at it closely.

▲ *This frog is well camouflaged against the stony ground. Can you name three other animals that use camouflage to catch their prey?*

Food chains

A food chain is a sequence of organisms that are eaten or eat each other within a particular habitat. Most plants and animals in a habitat are part of more than one food chain because they eat more than one type of food. This means that you could draw many different food chains within one habitat.

Plant producers

Plants are always at the start of a food chain because they are the only organisms that can make their own food within their bodies. They are called producers. Plants collect energy from the Sun through their leaves and use it to make their own sugary food from air and water. This process is called photosynthesis. Plants mainly store the sugary food in their leaves. This food and nutrients that plants take up from the soil through their roots help plants to grow. Most plants are food for another organism.

Animal consumers

Animals cannot make their own food. Animals are called consumers because they consume (eat) plants or other animals. Herbivores (plant-eaters) eat a plant's leaves or stems and get energy from

▲ Branches grow at different places on a tree so that their leaves do not overlap too much. This makes sure that each leaf can catch as much sunlight as possible.

This bird has caught a caterpillar. Caterpillars eat leaves. How does that help the bird get the energy that it needs?

the sugary food stored there. Many herbivores, such as rabbits, will be eaten as prey by carnivores (flesh-eaters), such as foxes and other predators. In this way, energy flows through the food chain and through the habitat.

How food chain diagrams work

Each organism in a food chain diagram is drawn as a link in a chain. A food chain starts with what gets eaten and arrows point towards the animals that do the eating. The arrows only go in one direction.

The animal at the other end of a food chain is an apex predator (top predator) and is not hunted or eaten by any other animals. Predators are carnivores. A lion is an apex predator. Can you think of three other animals that are apex predators?

Fox

is eaten by

is eaten by

Rabbit

is eaten by

is eaten by

is eaten by

Grass

Food chain diagrams

Here are two ways of drawing a food chain from a meadow habitat. Which of these organisms is a producer and which are consumers?

Make a poster

Design and make a poster of a simple food chain for a habitat of your choice. Use pictures you have drawn, cut out from magazines or downloaded from the Internet. Or you could draw your own images using a computer paint programme.

Life in a desert

Hot deserts cover about one third of the Earth's land surface, but they are difficult habitats to live in. Deserts have little or no soil. They can be rocky or sandy, but all deserts are very dry. They may get no rain for months on end. As a result, fewer organisms live in deserts than in many other habitats. Those that do live there have special adaptations to help them survive.

Desert plants

Most organisms must have water to survive. Many cactus plants have thick stems that can expand and store water. Cacti have sharp spikes that stop animals from stealing their water. As they do not have flat leaves, cacti use their stems to trap sunlight for photosynthesis. Some desert plants, such as desert grasses, have very long, shallow roots that spread across a wide area to catch any rain that drains into the soil.

▲ Camels eat desert plants. They do not store water in their humps. Instead, they use them to store fat from their food. They turn the fat into energy when they need it.

These saguaro cacti are in a desert ▶ in Arizona in the USA. If you could step into the habitat in this picture, how do you think you would feel?

This is a horned viper snake. It moves by wiggling sideways. This means only a small part of its body touches the sand at a time. Why does it need to keep off the sand?

Desert animals

A desert food chain starts with a desert plant, such as a cactus. Some insects and bats eat nectar from the centre of cacti flowers. Animals, such as beetles, mice and birds, eat fruits and seeds from the cacti. In turn, predators such as owls, lizards and tarantula spiders eat these desert consumers. Then larger predators, including mountain lions, snakes and jackals, eat those predators. As well as food energy, many desert animals also need the liquid they get from their prey.

To survive the desert heat, many animals, such as gerbils, live under rocks or burrow under the sand where it is cooler. Woodpeckers make their nests and shelter in cacti by boring holes in their thick trunks. Most desert animals also feed or hunt after dark when it is cooler. In the daytime, all that can be seen of them are their tracks.

Internet games

Play a game to find out how much you know about the animals that live in desert habitats. Go to the http://www.activescience-gsk.com website. Click on the 'Humans and Animal Habitats' section. Then play the desert game.

Life in a rainforest

Tropical rainforests are very thick forests found around the Equator, the hottest region on Earth. As well as being very warm, rainforests have rain almost every day. The warm, wet climate provides ideal living conditions for many organisms. The rainforest is home to more than half of the world's animals!

This rainforest is in Brazil in South America. Toucans live in South American rainforests. What food types do you think they eat?

Rainforest plants

The trees in a rainforest grow up to 50 metres high, which is as tall as ten double-decker buses stacked on top of each other. They grow to these heights because they have plenty of warmth, sunlight and water. Their high, leaf-covered branches shade the ground below. Some plants, such as shrubs and large-leafed palm trees, can still catch enough light to survive on the forest floor. Other plants, such as vines, wrap their stems around the trunks of the trees and slowly grow up towards the light.

Many rainforest trees have huge roots that spread above the ground. Can you describe how their shape helps to prop up these giant trees?

Rainforest destruction

Over the past 150 years, more than half of the world's trees have been cut down. Use the Internet to find out why. What are the wood and land used for? What happens to the animals when the trees are gone?

Rainforest animals

The rich variety of plant life in a rainforest is the basis for many different food chains. Millions of different insects feed on rainforest plants. In turn, the insects provide food for many animals, including the red-eyed tree frog. Colourful parrots have big strong beaks to crack and eat nuts. Many types of monkey climb high to feed on fruit and leaves.

The smaller plant-eaters provide food for large birds of prey, such as the harpy eagle. Jaguars, leopards and giant anteaters are some of the other predators that feed on rainforest animals. Draw a simple rainforest food chain.

What adaptations does this howler monkey have to help it move, live and feed in the rainforest habitat? How do its long arms, legs and tail help?

Investigating habitats

You may not be able to visit a real desert or rainforest but there are many habitats closer to home to investigate. Even in towns and cities there are parks and gardens, hedges, patches of wasteland, and old walls that make habitats for many animals and plants.

Play it safe

• When you have chosen a habitat to study, check it is safe and always go with an adult or tell an adult where you are going.

• Always wash your hands after visiting a habitat, especially after handling animals, water or soil.

Planning and predicting

Before you go, try to predict which organisms you might find in your chosen habitat. Describe and think about the conditions of the habitat to help with your predictions. For example, among the ivy on an old wall you would expect to find snails. As well as shelter and plant food, the snail gets minerals for building its shell from the wall itself.

What to take

Here is a list of items to take with you:

• Notebook, pens and pencils, and plain paper for sketches.

• Tweezers or a scoop.

• Trays or jars with perforated lids to hold invertebrates. Holes in the lid enable the creatures inside to breathe.

• Hand lens or a magnifier.

• Identification book or identification key for plants and animals.

• Binoculars and camera (with flash and close-up lens) if you have them.

What else would you take in your bag?

Country code

While out and about, try not to disturb wildlife or damage the habitat.

• If you collect creatures to study always handle them gently and put them back where you found them.

• Do not pick wild flowers. Draw or photograph them instead.

• Do not trample plants.

• Close gates behind you.

Can you think why each of these country code rules is important?

Count the animals, such as snails and spiders, that you find in a flower bed, and make a bar chart like the one below with your results. Which animal was the most common in your survey?

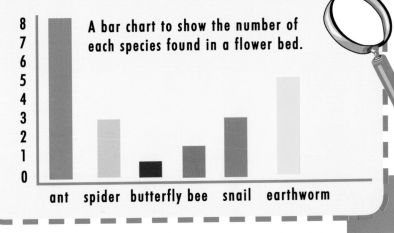

A bar chart to show the number of each species found in a flower bed.

8
7
6
5
4
3
2
1
0

ant   spider   butterfly   bee   snail   earthworm

How to investigate

Write a description of the habitat, including the plants and animals. Sketch the habitat. Label mini habitats found within the main habitat. Identify as many organisms as you can and record your results in a notebook.

Collect invertebrates and draw sketches or take photos of them. If there are plants or animals that you cannot identify, take a photo of them and ask an adult to help you identify them after you have completed the investigation.

My invertebrate identification chart

six legs

eight legs

no legs

more than eight legs

◀ *Before your investigation, make an identification chart. You can build on this simple start.*

Recording results

When you return, you will need to organise your findings. Think how to record and present the information. You could write a report, beginning with the conditions in the habitat and describing how the plants, invertebrates and vertebrates are adapted for life there. Or you could record your findings in a tally chart or a bar chart like the one on this page.

Exploring woodlands

Some woodlands have trees with broad, flat leaves such as oak, beech and ash. These are deciduous trees and they lose all their leaves in autumn. Coniferous woodlands have trees like pine, spruce and fir, whose dark, needle-like leaves cover the tree all year round. The ground below coniferous trees is too dark and damp for many other plants to grow. As conifer leaves or needles are not good for animals to eat, these woodlands usually contain less wildlife than deciduous woodlands.

Woodland insects

Hundreds of different types of caterpillar (the larvae of butterflies and moths) feast on the leaves of deciduous trees. On the woodland floor, woodlice feed on rotting wood, and groups of ants work together to catch caterpillars. In coniferous woodlands, only the larvae of the pine sawfly can feed on the spiky leaves.

▶ Centipedes have a long, flat body to squeeze under leaves on a woodland floor. They eat worms, insects and slugs.

▲ Woodpeckers peck holes in a tree's trunk to get at insects beneath the bark.

A branching key

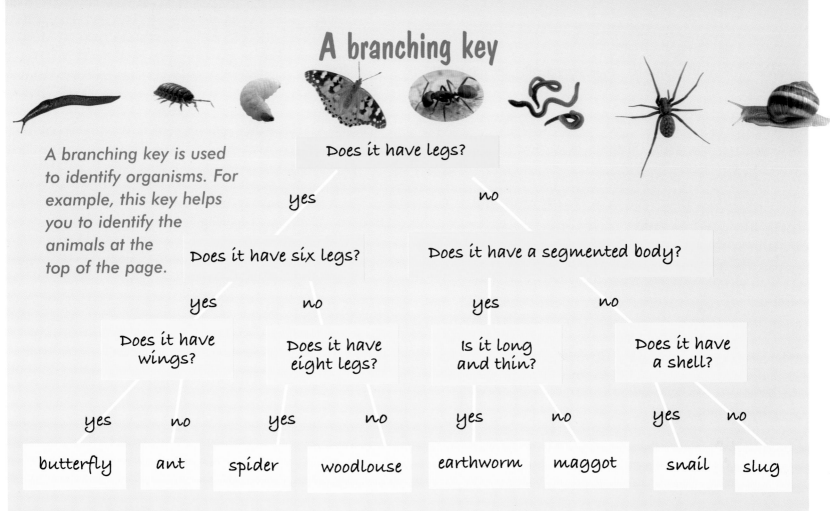

A branching key is used to identify organisms. For example, this key helps you to identify the animals at the top of the page.

Does it have legs?

yes — no

Does it have six legs? — Does it have a segmented body?

yes — no — yes — no

Does it have wings? — Does it have eight legs? — Is it long and thin? — Does it have a shell?

yes — no — yes — no — yes — no — yes — no

butterfly — ant — spider — woodlouse — earthworm — maggot — snail — slug

Pick an animal from the top, answer the questions in order and see if the key works.

Woodland birds

Most woodlands are full of birds. Some eat seeds, berries or insects, while others, such as owls, eat other birds or small woodland mammals. Wrens and blue tits search for insects among the leaves. Coniferous trees have seeds that grow in cones, rather than in nuts and berries. Crossbills are birds that have twisted beaks adapted for pulling the seeds out from the cones.

Woodland mammals

Squirrels have large front teeth to break into the hard shells of the nuts they feed on. In some woodlands, the pine marten – a weasel-like animal – lives in tree holes and eats eggs, birds and other mammals. On the woodland floor, mice and rabbits feed on leaves and seeds, and deer feed on grasses and ferns. Badgers live in tunnels and emerge at night to eat beetles, slugs and worms.

Exploring a pond

A pond is an area of fresh water that does not flow, unlike rivers and streams which are always moving. Whether it is large or small, there are several zones of life in a pond habitat. Organisms can be found in the shallow water at the edge of a pond, on the surface of the water and under the water.

Pond plants

At the edge of a pond, plants such as reeds and irises grow. Their roots push down into the mud and their leaves and flowers are held above the water. The large, flat leaves of the water lily float on the surface of the pond. Its roots are in the mud and its long, air-filled stems float the leaves to the surface to get the light they need.

Pond sweeping

Use a pond net to sweep through pond water, near plants at the edge, and through mud. Plan what you would need to contain your catches and to observe them. Download and construct a pondwatch bug dial from http://www.wwtlearn.org.uk/worksheets/worksheet-bug_dial.pdf to help identify your findings. Which of the animals' features help them survive in a pond? Remember not to go too near the water's edge and always have an adult with you.

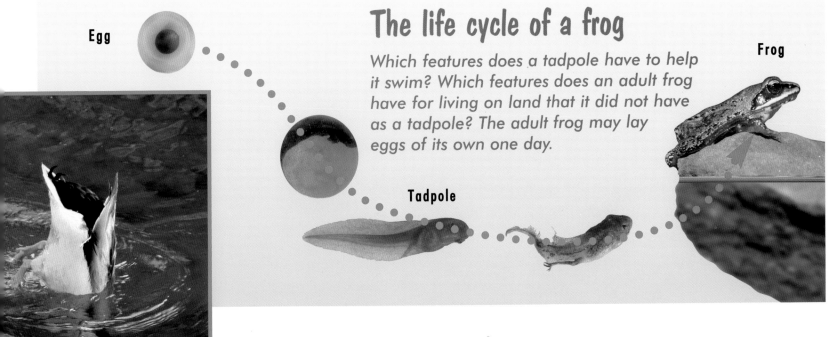

The life cycle of a frog

Egg

Frog

Which features does a tadpole have to help it swim? Which features does an adult frog have for living on land that it did not have as a tadpole? The adult frog may lay eggs of its own one day.

Tadpole

▲ A duck is adapted to its pond habitat. It has oiled feathers to make it waterproof. These ducks are feeding underwater. How do a duck's webbed feet help it to swim?

Animals on or above the water

Birds, such as ducks and swans, swim across a pond. There are also many insects that use the surface of the water. A pond skater has long, thin legs and a body so light that it can skate across the pond. Water boatmen have legs like paddles which allow them to swim. They carry a bubble of air to breathe when they dive to catch tadpoles, small fish and insects. Larger insects, such as damselflies and dragonflies, fly above ponds and swallow up tiny insects.

Animals under the water

Under the water you may find a great pond snail, which floats upside down at the water's surface, and grates off bits of plants with its rough tongue. Pond fish include sticklebacks and minnows. Their streamlined bodies help them to move smoothly through the water.

▲ A diving beetle kills prey by biting with its huge jaws.

Habitats at different times

Habitats change through the seasons of the year, and this has an effect on the organisms that live there. The animals that roam, feed and hunt in a habitat during the night are also different from the animals that are active in that habitat during the daytime.

Night and day

Owls and bats are nocturnal animals. This means that they are active at night. Owls have large eyes to help them see small animals in dim light, and they have sensitive hearing that pinpoints the location of mice and small rabbits.

Bats find their food by using echolocation. First they make a high-pitched sound. When the sound hits an insect, the echo bounces back. The bat's large ears track the echoes so the bat can follow and catch its prey.

Spring and summer

In spring and summer, most habitats are full of life. The warmer, wetter days of spring encourage new plants to grow from seeds that have spent winter underground. This is also the time when insects and other herbivores (plant-eating

If birds hunt insects during the daytime, how does hunting at night make life easier for the bat?

◀ Squirrels hoard nuts during the spring and summer when food is plentiful.

animals) are born, because there are plenty of plants for them to feed on. This in turn makes spring and summer the time that carnivores (flesh-eating animals) have their young, because there are plenty of new animals for them to eat.

Autumn and winter

In autumn, many plants and trees bear fruit and nuts, but they also begin to lose their leaves. By winter, it is very cold and there is little food about. To keep warm during the winter, some animals grow thicker fur. Squirrels survive the winter months by eating nuts that they have hoarded.

Some animals, such as hedgehogs, hibernate. They fatten up over the summer and then in the late autumn they go into a safe, quiet place where they can sleep. Their body temperature drops and their heartbeat and breathing slow down. They use up very little energy until they are ready to become active again in spring.

▲ Lions are carnivores. They have their young when young antelopes and zebra are born. This supplies the cubs with a good diet.

Animal clues

We can tell when nocturnal animals have been in a habitat by the evidence they leave behind. Compile a tracker's guide to nocturnal animals. Look at page 24 of this website to help start you off http://www.face-online.org.uk/resources/biodiversity/introduction.pdf

◄ Hedgehogs hibernate during the winter months.

Changing habitats

Some habitats change naturally over time. For example, a tree will die and decay when it reaches a very old age. But many habitats are damaged or destroyed by people. This has a serious effect on the organisms that live there.

Causes of habitat loss

Many habitats, including forests, marshes and grasslands, have been cleared. This makes way for farms, roads, factories, airports and other buildings. People also cut down forests and use the wood for making paper or for building houses.

River, pond and coastal habitats are often damaged by pollution. The water is poisoned or made dirty by pollutants such as sewage, factory waste and litter. Pollution is also caused by farm sprays that wash into rivers from fields.

▲ Water plants often die if the water they grow in is polluted. Which animals in a fresh water food chain would be affected if the plants die?

Have your say

Jake is worried that a precious woodland is going to be destroyed by his council in order to build a car park. He has written a letter to the council. What do you think he would have said?

Effects of habitat loss

When a habitat is damaged or destroyed, the animals that lived there can be threatened with extinction. They do not have a place to find food, keep safe or to have young.

Some animals are able to adapt and find new habitats. For example, when woodlands and meadows are cleared, some foxes come to towns to search for food in tips or dustbins. Other animals may starve or freeze, or die out because predators can more easily capture their young.

Interdependency

A habitat and the plants and animals that live in it depend on each other in many ways. This is called interdependency. A change to just one type of animal can affect the whole habitat. For example, when large numbers of sea otters were hunted off the coast of North America, the sea urchins that they usually eat greatly increased in number. The sea urchins devoured and almost destroyed the kelp (seaweed) forest habitat which is home and food to a variety of fish and many other animals.

This coral reef is alive and healthy. It is home to a wide variety of plant and animal life. ▶

Corals are animals that build coral reefs, usually in tropical seas. Coral reefs provide a habitat for thousands of sea organisms but they are very sensitive to pollution. A slight change in temperature or the saltiness of the water is enough to kill, or bleach, a coral reef.

◀ *This coral reef habitat has been bleached and killed by pollution and by an increase in the temperature of the seawater. The seawater has become warmer as a result of global warming. Compare this coral reef to the one above. How has the coral bleaching affected the animal and plant life?*

Protecting habitats

Across the world, there are individuals and groups of people working in conservation. They want to protect and save threatened habitats.

Who helps habitats?

Some conservation groups are large organisations, such as Friends of the Earth and the WWF (World Wide Fund for Nature). They may work with governments to create nature reserves or national parks. These are areas of habitat where it is against the law to cut down trees and other plants, or create pollution. They are sometimes fenced off to keep the animals safe. Conservation groups also make posters and raise awareness about the threats to world habitats.

Take action! Get involved or even organise a litter clean-up in a habitat near your home. But never touch anything dangerous or sharp.

Organisations

Use the Internet to gather information about an organisation that tries to protect wild habitats and educate people about them. This could be an international group, such as the WWF, or a British one, such as the National Trust or the Countryside Alliance. Find out about what they do.

How we can protect habitats?

Individual people can make a difference. You could cycle, walk or go to school in a bus or a friend's car to reduce air pollution caused by car fumes. Avoid dropping litter or waste and if you spot serious pollution, such as oil in a stream, report it to your local council.

If you are concerned about world habitats, you could raise money to donate to a conservation organisation, perhaps by doing a sponsored swim or by holding a bring-and-buy sale at school.

Make a habitat!

Why not design and plan a school wildlife garden? It could be large with a pond or small using a container or even a 'grow bag' from a garden centre. You could use the Internet to find out which plants attract wildlife, such as butterflies, to a garden. What will your wildlife garden look like? Where will you put it? When it is finished, you could keep a record of what animals live in or visit it, and observe how it changes.

▲ These students are sowing seeds to create a new garden habitat to attract wildlife, such as birds, butterflies and other mini-beasts.

Glossary

adaptation
a feature of an organism that helps it survive in its environment, such as a body part, body shape or behaviour.

amphibian
an animal such as frog, toad or newt that hatches and develops underwater but lives mainly on land as an adult.

bird
a vertebrate that has feathers, wings and lays eggs.

camouflage
markings or colouring that help an animal to blend in with its surroundings.

carnivore
an animal that eats other animals.

classify
to group organisms or other things together according to their similarities and differences.

conditions
describes the features of a habitat that make it what it is, for example how light, dark, hot, cold, dry or wet a habitat is.

cone
a part of a conifer tree that contains seeds.

coniferous
trees that have needle-shaped leaves that are never lost all at once.

conservation
protecting and preserving plants, animals and their habitats.

consumer
an organism that consumes (eats) plants or other animals.

deciduous
trees that lose all of their leaves at once.

echolocation
a system that bats use to find their way around and catch food in the dark. They make high-pitched sounds, and then interpret the echoes.

energy
the ability to do work. People get energy from food.

Equator
an imaginary line around the centre of the Earth.

extinction
when a species (type) of plant or animal dies out completely.

fish
a vertebrate that lives in water, has scales and breathes through gills.

herbivore
an animal that eats only plants.

hibernate	to spend winter in a deep sleep.
interdependency	the way that organisms in a habitat, and the habitat itself, need each other for survival.
invertebrate	an animal without a backbone.
larvae	the young of some animals. Larvae hatch out of the eggs of insects such as moths and butterflies and gradually develop into adults.
mammal	an animal that has hair or fur and feeds its young on milk, such as rabbits, cats and humans.
nectar	a sugary liquid that plants make to attract insects. Insects eat nectar.

nocturnal	animals that are active at night.
nutrient	a substance that nourishes plants and animals, keeps them healthy and helps them grow.
organism	a living thing, such as a plant or animal.

photosynthesis	the process by which plants make food from air and water using the energy in sunlight.
pollution	something that poisons or damages a habitat.
predator	an animal that hunts and catches other animals for food.
prey	an animal that is hunted and caught by other animals for food.
producer	something that can make its own food. A plant is a producer.
reproductive	to do with reproduction. In reproduction, organisms produce offspring (babies).
reptile	an animal that has hard, scaly skin and hatches from soft eggs, such as snakes and lizards.
streamlined	a body shape that helps objects, including animals, move faster through air or water.
temperature	a measure of how hot or cold something is.
vertebrate	an animal with a backbone.

For teachers and parents

This book is designed to support and extend the learning objectives for Unit 4B of the QCA Science Schemes of Work.

It is never difficult to get children interested in animals and their habitats, and in this unit they get the chance to explore the ways in which animals are adapted to their habitats. They will learn about interdependency – the way that plants, animals and the habitat in which they live are inextricably linked and rely on each other for health and survival.

Throughout this book and throughout their own investigative work, children should be aware that science is based on evidence and they should have the opportunity to:

- Turn questions into an investigation.
- Predict results.
- Understand the need to collect sufficient evidence.
- Understand the need to conduct a fair test.
- Choose and use appropriate measuring or investigation equipment.
- Record results using tables and bar charts, sometimes using ICT.
- Interpret evidence by making observations, comparisons and conclusions using scientific language.

There are opportunities for cross-curricular work in literacy, numeracy, art, design technology and ICT.

SUGGESTED FURTHER ACTIVITIES

Pages 4 - 5 What is a habitat?

To help children understand what a habitat is, they could group habitats of similar scale or diversity, either from a list on the board, or using pictures.

The Planet ARKive website (http://www.planetarkive.org) has lots of child-friendly information about habitats and free photos for the children to download and use for their own displays.

The children can continue adjective work on habitats by coming up with some of their own words to describe a familiar habitat, or one that they have researched. They could create adjective word banks for different types of habitat.

Pages 6 - 7 Classifying living things

Get the children thinking about classifying by asking them to group sets of photos according to connections or similarities they find between them.

To help the children with animal classification, they could sort pictures of mammals, reptiles, birds, amphibians and fish into their groups. Or they could play a game of 'Who Am I?' (using yellow stickies always works if you do not have headbands) where the person guessing has to ask questions using the classification terminology, such as 'Do I lay eggs?', 'Do I have fur on my body?'.

The children could try to identify which tree a leaf comes from by using a key, and learn how observable features can be used to construct keys for other flowering plants.

Pages 8 - 9 Finding food in habitats

The children could create a poster or labelled drawing showing an animal of their choice and explaining its adaptations for finding food in its habitat. They could research a new animal at http://www.bbc.co.uk/nature/reallywild/amazing/

Pages 10 - 11 Food chains

Ask the children to construct a food chain with themselves in it, either using just words or pictures too, to encourage them to think of themselves as part of the animal world.

The children could make a mobile of a food chain of their choice, from a particular habitat.

Pages 12 - 13 Life in a desert

Print off some pictures of desert plants and animals, and ask the children to write their own captions for the pictures.

The children could write a shape or acrostic poem about an animal in a desert, or other exciting new habitat. Or they could create their own myth, such as how the cactus got its spikes.

Find a world map and help the children to locate some of the world's largest deserts and find out more about one of them.

Pages 14 - 15 Life in a rainforest
Try to obtain a rainforest recording or simply ask children to imagine what a rainforest would sound like with all the animal life in it. Using instruments and sound objects, encourage the children to create some rainforest rhythms. The children could then perform their particular rhythm to the rest of the class.

Children could write a newspaper report or article for a travel journal about a scary encounter in a rainforest.

Visit a zoo that offers rainforest experiences and workshops for children, and which also discusses wider issues such as deforestation. For example, Bristol Zoo provides these facilities.

Pages 16 - 17 Investigating habitats
Children can use mathematics when investigating habitats. They could calculate the area of a habitat using squared paper. They could sample a measured area, for example of a field, and count the number of invertebrates within it. That figure can be used to estimate the total number of invertebrates in the whole field.

Children could be an 'invertebrate estate agent' for an animal of their choice. They would need to research the animal's needs and then produce an advert to entice it to move into their new habitat.

When investigating a habitat, it is a good opportunity to look at an Ordnance Survey map of the route to be taken and to draw a map or plan of the habitat itself. Labelling maps carefully will also help the children to write up a report later. They could be encouraged to mark on where they found or saw particular animals or plants.

Pages 18 - 19 Exploring woodlands
Children can carry out 'virtual' habitat investigations at http://www.naturegrid.org.uk/explorer/index.html or use the site to compare animals found in a local habitat with the habitats they can explore here.

Pages 20 - 21 Exploring a pond
Help the children to build a branching database to identify animals in a pond. Information and help on using ICT in schools can be found at http://schools.becta.org.uk/

Children could think about water pollution while doing a pond dipping exercise. They could take a sample of water and compare it to tap water when they get back to school to see how clean tap water looks. This also reinforces the importance of washing hands afterwards.

Pages 22 - 23 Habitats at different times
Children could find out about other animal adaptations for nocturnal life, such as the centipede that uses antennae to feel and find prey, or animals that can see in the dark.

To extend the idea of habitats changing with seasons, children could do some work on bird migration, and plot migration routes of some bird species. There are useful resources and downloadable maps at http://www.wwtlearn.org.uk/index0.html?lesson_plans/heading_south. htm&2 and http://www.rspb.org.uk/youth/learn/catalogue/science/ migratory_paths.asp

Pages 24 - 25 Changing habitats
Children could write a personal piece about how they feel about habitat destruction and what it is doing to the world's wildlife.

Lichen is a good indicator of habitat health; bearded lichen only grows in clean air. Children could become 'pollution detectives' and check which lichens are seen in three different places when they do their habitat studies.

Pages 26-27 – Protecting habitats
Children could research an animal success story, where an animal near to extinction has been brought back from the brink, possibly after a successful captive breeding programme, such as the Californian condor, the golden lion tamarin monkey or the Indian rhino.

Index